IF PREHISTORIC BEASTS WERE HERE TODAY

HUNTERS of the Deep

Thanks to the creative team:

Senior Editor:Alice Peebles
Consultant: Neil Clark
Fact checking: Kate Mitchell
Design: www.collaborate.agency

First published in Great Britain in 2016
by Hungry Tomato Ltd
PO Box 181
Edenbridge
Kent, TN8 9DP

A CIP catalogue record for this book is
available from the British Library.

ISBN 978-1-910684-75-7

Printed and bound in China

Discover more at
www.hungrytomato.com

IF PREHISTORIC BEASTS WERE HERE TODAY

HUNTERS of the Deep

by Matthew Rake

Illustrated by Simon Mendez

HUNGRY TOMATO™

WARNING!
These extinct beasts are not alive today. But just imagine if they were...

CONTENTS

THE BIG, THE BAD AND THE UGLY

We all know that some very ugly, very scary dinosaurs ruled the Earth for over 100 million years. But they weren't the only creatures on the planet. Before – and after – the dinosaurs, there were other animals every bit as spine-chilling. Can you imagine what the world would be like if they came back to life? Well, you are about to find out...

All life started in the sea – and that's where the first big, scary animals appeared, too. About 475 million years ago, there were massive sea scorpions with claws the size of tennis rackets, and creatures in shells called nautiloids, the size of crocodiles.

The first dinosaurs evolved 240–230 million years ago, but they didn't rule the world straightaway. They couldn't – they were 'only' 2–3 m (6–10 ft) long, and some **just twice the size of chickens**. Even when dinosaurs had become ginormous, they had to watch out for crocs like *Sarcosuchus*. Four times as heavy as today's crocs, it liked a dinosaur for dinner.

Nautiloids

Liopleurodon

Kimmerosaurus

In the seas, the top predators were reptiles such as the pliosaurs. A mighty specimen was the sleek and deadly 6-m-long (21-ft) *Liopleurodon* (left), here shown grabbing a plesiosaur called *Kimmerosaurus*. Find out about the terrifying deeds of the **biggest pliosaur of all**, *Pliosaurus funkei* (aka Predator X), on page 16.

Mammals started evolving at the same time as dinosaurs. But they kept a low profile while the dinosaurs were around. For about 160 million years, most mammals were shrew-sized – any larger and they would have been gobbled up by hungry carnivorous dinosaurs.

After the dinosaurs died out, **mammals grew to massive proportions.** *Chalicotherium* (left) lived from about 28 million to 4 million years ago and stood about 2.75 m (9 ft) tall. Some mammals even evolved into sea creatures. Whales were once land-based mammals that started swimming in the seas to catch fish. On page 26 you can meet the biggest whale ever: *Livyatan*.

So, prepare to plunge into the ancient oceans to discover not only giant sea scorpions and nautiloids, but also truly epic marine monsters, such as armour-plated Dunkleosteus (below). And if you think today's killer whales and great whites are dangerous... well, they are peace-loving pussycats compared to their awesome ancestors.

Chalicotherium

If you've got the courage to witness the invasion of the prehistoric sea brutes, read on... just be prepared for some truly bizarre and scary encounters between humans (or animals) and these now-extinct beasts.

Dunkleosteus

7

BIG NIPPER
SEA SCORPION OR EURYPTERID

Let's face it, we are all a little frightened of scorpions – even though they are only a few centimetres long. Can you imagine scorpions bigger than an adult human? No? Well, meet the modern scorpion's bigger, badder prehistoric ancestors: the sea scorpions or eurypterids. They swam through ancient oceans, and scuttled across sea floors, terrorizing every other living thing they came in contact with.

The sea scorpion chased down prey quickly with the help of its long tail and paddle-like swimming legs. Then it would go in for the kill with its huge claws. These were the size of tennis rackets and covered with deadly spines, perfect for holding the unfortunate victim against the sea floor, and then slicing and shredding it! The only thing it was missing was an underwater chopping board.

What if sea scorpions lived today? You'd have to feel sorry for the diver here. But if he's a strong swimmer he'd probably lose no more than a flipper – surely?

EURYPTERID
PRONOUNCED
You-RIP-ter-id

LIVED
Seas worldwide,
around 467–250 million
years ago

LENGTH
Up to 2.5 m (8 ft)

FOSSIL FINDS

What's New York famous for? Yeah, a city full of skyscrapers, Broadway theatres and Fifth Avenue shops. But New York state has one big claim to fame: hundreds of eurypterid finds, including the first one ever, in 1818. In fact, the sea scorpion is the designated state fossil.

TENTACLED TERROR
CAMEROCERAS

The nautiloids of today swim in the seas around Australia and the Philippines. They live in shells, look pretty and are only about 20 cm (8 in) long. They certainly can't do any harm to a sizeable creature. Well, check out this nautiloid – it's called *Cameroceras*. It's longer than your average minivan and it's a ruthless predator – as this croc would surely admit.

Cameroceras is using its tangle of grasping tentacles to drag its prey towards its beak. And you don't want to go anywhere near the beak. It can crunch straight through hard shells – so the armoured scales of this small croc aren't going to give it too much trouble. And worse is to come. Nautiloids of today have a toothed tongue known as a 'radula'. This allows them to scrape and cut out the soft fleshy parts of its victim. Scientists think *Cameroceras* would have had exactly the same tongue. Imagine if *Cameroceras* lived alongside today's sea creatures. It's hard to pity a vicious creature like a croc, but in this case it perhaps deserves a little sympathy.

CAMEROCERAS
PRONOUNCED
Cam-eh-RO-seh-rass

LIVED
Northern seas,
470–451 million
years ago

LENGTH
Up to 6 m (20 ft)

HEAVILY ARMED

Today's nautiloids have up to 94 tentacles. Why do they need so many? Some tentacles are used to touch and sense chemicals. Some bring food to its beak. These are coated with a sticky substance to help the food stay on!

PART BEAST, PART BATTLESHIP

DUNKLEOSTEUS

This dolphin might look as if it is getting away from the huge, superpowerful fish, *Dunkleosteus*. But bear in mind *Dunkleosteus* does not actually have to catch the dolphin. All it needs to do is get close enough to open its mouth. It can do this in one-fiftieth of a second – so quickly that it creates a suction force to pull the dolphin back into its mouth. And once it has its prey in its jaws, there is no hope. *Dunkleosteus'* bite force has been estimated at 5,000 Newtons (1,100 lb) – that's more powerful than the bite of a lion, tiger or hyena!

Not surprisingly, *Dunkleosteus* was an apex predator in its time – this means that no other creature preyed upon it. However, *Dunkleosteus* did have to watch out for one other animal – fellow *Dunkleosteus*. Some fossils show injuries created by the razor-sharp plating of other *Dunkleosteus*. Maybe they fought over territory – or, more probably, they were simply trying to eat each other.

DUNKLEOSTEUS
PRONOUNCED
Dun-kul-OSS-tee-us

LIVED
Shallow seas worldwide,
380–360 million years
ago

LENGTH
Up to 10 m (33 ft)

WEIGHT
3–4 tonnes
(3.3–4.4 US tons)

ARMOUR-PLATED

Dunkleosteus was one of a group of armoured skinned fish known as 'placoderms', which means 'plate-skinned' in Greek. Its skull was about 1.3 m (4 ft) wide and had armour-plating all around it. The plating was up to 5 cm (2 in) thick, but at the jaws this thinned down to razor-sharp edges. These made perfect blades for crushing fish.

STRETCH-NECKED SAVAGE
TANYSTROPHEUS

Who needs a fishing rod when you have a neck 3 m (10 ft) long? This is *Tanystropheus* and today scientists believe its super-stretched neck helped it to catch fish. However, when Italian palaeontologist Francesco Bassani first discovered *Tanystropheus* fossils in 1886, he couldn't believe any animal could have such a long neck. So he decided he must have found the wing bones of a giant pterosaur – the flying reptiles that lived during the days of the dinosaurs.

Although we now know *Tanystropheus* definitely didn't fly, we are still not sure whether it lived in the water or the land. Scientists now think it probably lived somewhere in between – near the shoreline. Its front legs are shorter than the back ones, which would have been perfect for leaning forward at the water's edge for feeding. It probably liked to feed at tidal pools, which would be restocked with new fish every time the tide came in. But it might have taken a dip in the sea if it saw some particularly juicy prey. Good thing *Tanystropheus* isn't around today to catch dogs going for a swim!

TANYSTROPHEUS
PRONOUNCED
Tan-ee-STROH-fee-us

LIVED
Shores of Europe,
215 million years ago

LENGTH
About 6 m (20 ft)

WEIGHT
140 kg (300 lb)

TALL TAIL

Tanystropheus' neck was about 3 m (10 ft), half its total length. Its tail was almost 2 m (6 ft 6 in) long, a third of its length. But its body was only about 1 m (3 ft 3 in) long, just one-sixth of its length.

LET'S GET FUNKEI
PLIOSAURUS FUNKEI

Check out this monster erupting out of the sea with a humpback whale in its jaws. This big bruiser of a reptile is *Pliosaurus funkei*. It lived at the time of the dinosaurs and you could call it the *Tyrannosaurus rex* of the seas. It measured up to 13 m (43 ft) – about the same length as your average bus. Its skull alone was bigger than a human and it contained teeth as long as carving knives.

Scientists think that most of the time *Pliosaurus funkei* cruised around just using its two front flippers. But for a torpedo-like assault like this, it also used its back flippers to gain extra speed and propel itself towards its giant prey. Of course, these days humpback whales have nothing to fear from any such random attacks – luckily for these peace-loving giants.

PLIOSAURUS FUNKEI
PRONOUNCED
Plio-SORE-us-FUNK-eye
LIVED
Arctic Ocean, 150 million years ago
LENGTH
10–13 m (33–43 ft),
skull: 2–2.5 m
(6 ft 6 in–8 ft)
WEIGHT
22.3 tonnes (24.5 US tons)

BIG PREY HUNTERS

Pliosaurs, with their massive jaws and teeth around 30 cm (12 in) long, evolved to capture large prey including other pliosaurs, plesiosaurs (see next page) and possibly giant fish such as *Leedsichthys* (see page 22).

3D JIGSAW

Scientists only discovered *Pliosaurus funkei* in 2006. That's when a huge pliosaur skeleton was found on the Arctic islands of Svalbard, Norway. At first, scientists couldn't tell what it was and called it "Predator X". There were around 20,000 fossil pieces and putting it together was like doing a gigantic 3D jigsaw. Eventually, in 2012, they announced they had found the biggest pliosaur of all time, naming it *Pliosaurus funkei*.

STICKING ITS NECK OUT
ELASMOSAURUS

This magnificent beast is really going the extra mile, isn't it? It's an *Elasmosaurus*, a member of the plesiosaur family of marine reptiles that lived from 200 million to around 66 million years ago. It has been described as 'a snake threaded through the shell of a turtle' but it certainly didn't have a shell. Its neck alone was about 7 m (23 ft), half the length of its entire body.

Scientists think it spent most of its time in the depths, so its heavy neck was buoyed up by the water. To eat, *Elasmosaurus* would swim up to a shoal of fish, probably from below to remain hidden, and then dart its head into the shoal to snatch fish. Its teeth were sharp and overlapped so that fish could not wriggle free. Then the prey would be swallowed whole, and begin the long journey down *Elasmosaurus*' neck.

The surfer here is probably not in too much danger, though. *Elasmosaurus*' teeth weren't designed for ripping into large prey. It's probably just coming up for air – or to find out what this alien creature is doing floating around on a piece of wood.

ELASMOSAURUS
PRONOUNCED
El-azz-mo-SORE-us

LIVED
North America,
80.5 million
years ago

LENGTH
Up to about
15 m (49 ft)

WEIGHT
2 tonnes (2.2 US tons)

A BIT OF A BONEHEAD

US scientist Edward Drinker Cope named the *Elasmosaurus* in 1868. Unfortunately, when he put the skeleton together, he placed the head on the tail! By getting the skull the wrong way round, the professor proved to be a bit of a bonehead himself. *Elasmosaurus* looks rather like *Tanystropheus* on page 14. But it lived about 125 million years later. And was a much bigger and more terrifying creature.

GIANT TOOTH

MEGALODON

In today's world, killer whales are the undisputed rulers of the oceans. They don't fear anyone – even great white sharks get taken out by killer whales. It's not hard to see why. They can grow up to 10 m (33 ft) long and weigh a whopping 10 tonnes (11 US tons). And their teeth can measure up to 10 cm (4 in). This unfortunate sea lion is going to feel them... unless the killer whale feels *Megalodon*'s teeth first!

Megalodon was the biggest shark ever, about 40 times heavier than a great white. Its teeth were razor-sharp and serrated like steak knives. What's more, they were 18 cm (7 in) long. Compare that with the great white's, which are a paltry 3 cm (1.2 in). Not surprising, then, that *Megalodon* means 'giant tooth' in Greek.

MEGALODON

PRONOUNCED
MEG-ah-low-don

LIVED
Oceans worldwide,
25–2.6 million years ago

LENGTH
About 16 m (52 ft)

WEIGHT
Up to 100 tonnes
(110 US tons)

STONE TONGUES

Before people understood what fossils were, it was thought that *Megalodon* teeth were the tips of dragons' tongues. But in 1667, Nicholas Steno, the Duke of Florence's physician, realized that they came from an extinct shark.

CAR CRUSHER!

It wasn't just the size of its teeth that made *Megalodon* so fearsome, it was the force with which it used them. In 2012, scientists estimated its bite was more than three times more powerful than that of *Tyrannosaurus rex*, and almost 50 times more than a lion's – enough to crush a small car, or indeed a killer whale.

BIG MOUTH
LEEDSICHTHYS

This fish might look terrifying, and it did have 40,000 teeth, but it wasn't a predatory animal. Like today's blue whale, *Leedsichthys* lived on zooplankton: tiny animals, including shrimp, fish and jellyfish, that float near the surface of the sea. To get as much zooplankton as possible, *Leedsichthys* opened its mouth wide, and only used the teeth to filter out the zooplankton from sea water. Still, these kids want to watch out – that mouth is over 2 m (6 ft 6 in) wide and they don't want to end up with the zooplankton!

Unfortunately, lots about *Leedsichthys* remains mysterious and scientists have continually changed their minds about how big it is. At the start of the 20th century, they thought it was 9 m (30 ft) long. But by the end of the century, they estimated it was more than 30 m (100 ft). Now it has been downsized to 16.5 m (54 ft). It won't surprise you that the Latin name of this creature is *Leedsichthys problematicus*. It has proved very problematicus indeed. But one thing is for certain, it is the biggest bony fish ever discovered. (*Megalodon* was bigger, but sharks have skeletons of cartilage not bone, so are not classified as bony fish).

LEEDSICHTHYS
PRONOUNCED
Leeds-ICK-thiss

LIVED
European and
South American seas,
165–155 million
years ago

LENGTH
up to 16.5 m (54 ft)

FACT TITLE

British farmer Alfred Nicholson Leeds first discovered *Leedsichthys* bones in a pit near Peterborough, England, in 1886. He soon discovered more fossils and started a profitable sideline in selling them to collectors and natural history museums.

A WHALE OF A TIME

LIVYATAN

Wow, this fishing boat has attracted an amazing catch. The ginormous creature is *Livyatan*, the biggest predatory whale ever known. It lived about 12 million years ago, and probably ate almost anything that came its way – other whales, as well as dolphins, porpoises, sharks, sea turtles, seals and sea birds, have been found at the site where the remains of *Livyatan* have been excavated. One thing is certain: it needed a lot food to keep its 15-m (50-ft) body going.

Scientists think it may have attacked from below, approaching from the murky depths and slamming into its target from underneath like a rocket fired from the sea floor. This has been called the 'Polaris attack', named after the submarine-launched missile. Now the fishermen on the boat have to hope that *Livyatan* won't find the tough rigging very appetizing and will head back down to the depths!

LIVYATAN
PRONOUNCED
Li-VIE-ah-tan

LIVED
Shores of
South America,
13–12 million years ago

LENGTH
About 15 m (50 ft);
skull 3 m (10 ft) long

HUGE TEETH

Livyatan is related to today's sperm whales, which roam the oceans looking for giant squid to eat. However, today's sperm whale is a pussycat in comparison. It has small teeth and feeds by opening its jaws quickly so its prey is sucked into its mouth. *Livyatan*'s mouth was full of huge teeth and it snatched its prey with a powerful bite, inflicting deep wounds, then tearing off flesh.

SUPER SNAPPER

XIPHACTINUS

Xiphactinus terrorized the seas at the end of the dinosaur era. Even though it wasn't the biggest marine animal, it was a great predator. So what did it have that other sea beasts didn't? First, with its powerful tail and wing-like fins, it was fast. With a top speed of about 60 km/h (37 mph), *Xiphactinus* could swim towards prey – or away from predators – quicker than virtually anything else in the seas at the time. Second, it had vicious, needle-like teeth, 6 cm (2.3 in) long and perfect for piercing scales and flesh.

However, it could not chew or slice off smaller pieces, so it ate fish whole. There are lots of fossils to prove this. Inside a 4-m (13-ft) fossil found in 1952 by Walter Sorensen in Kansas, USA, there is a perfectly preserved 1.8-m (6-ft) *Gillicus* fish. Scientists think the *Gillicus*, in a desperate attempt to escape, ripped open the *Xiphactinus*' stomach and damaged some of its vital organs.

So this *Xiphactinus* better watch out for the swordfish. Let's face it, it doesn't want that sword-like bill flailing around in its stomach.

XIPHACTINUS

PRONOUNCED
Zih-fak-TIE-nuss

LIVED
Seas around
North America,
Europe, Australia,
100–66 million
years ago

LENGTH
4–6 m (13–20 ft)

UNDER WATER

Many *Xiphactinus* fossils have been found in Kansas, USA. So how did lots of fish fossils end up in the middle of the USA? When *Xiphactinus* lived, the prehistoric Western Interior Seaway covered much of what is now North America.

COMPLETE SKELETON

The Rocky Mountain Dinosaur Resource Center in Colorado, USA, is home to the biggest complete *Xiphactinus* skeleton. It measures 5.6 m (18 ft 4 in), and it took three experts three years to assemble.

TIMELINE

CAMEROCERAS

Named after the Greek for 'chambered horn'

Nautiloids get their name from the Greek 'nautilos' for sailor. The Greek philosopher and scientist Aristotle was one of the first people to study nautiloids.

DUNKLEOSTEUS

Named after its discoverer David Dunkle and *osteon,* the Greek for 'bone'

Heavy *Dunkleosteus* was probably not a fast swimmer. So it probably went after slow prey or used ambush tactics.

TANYSTROPHEUS

Named after the Greek for 'long vertebra' (spinal bone)

A 5-m (16-ft) life-like robotic *Tanystropheus* was installed at Youth Park swimming pool in Taipei in 2013 – and swimmers can actually ride it. Its creator, Masamichi Hayashi, has also made a robotic shark, whale, manatee and sea turtle.

EURYPTERIDS

Named after the Greek for 'wide wing'

Sea scorpions or eurypterids lived for over 200 million years, longer than the dinosaurs. Some 250 species are known.

LEEDSICHTHYS

Named after Alfred Leeds and 'ichthys', the Greek for 'fish'

A tooth found in one *Leedsichthys* fossil proves that it was attacked, or at least scavenged after its death, by the vicious crocodile-like reptile *Metriorhynchus.*

470 MILLION YEARS AGO > > >

Around 230 million years ago: First dinosaurs evolve > > >

ELASMOSAURUS

Named after the Greek for 'ribbon lizard'

The group known as elasmosaurids ate stones as well as fish! Hundreds of them have been found in the stomachs of elasmosaurid fossils. Maybe the stones helped grind down the fish they ate, or perhaps they helped its balance.

XIPHACTINUS

Named after the Latin and Greek for 'sword ray'

Xiphactinus might have been a lethal predator, but it was also prey for larger fish. A fossil of the prehistoric shark *Cretoxyrhina* has the scattered bones of *Xiphactinus* inside it.

MEGALODON

Named after the Greek for 'giant tooth'

Scientists have had to estimate the size of *Megalodon* from its teeth and vertebrae. The rest of a shark's skeleton is made up of soft cartilage which doesn't fossilize well.

PLIOSAURUS FUNKEI

Named after the Greek for 'more lizard', and Bjørn Funke who discovered it

Pliosaurs were massive reptiles that swam the Jurassic seas. There are five other known species of *Pliosaurus*.

LIVYATAN

Scientists originally called the creature Leviathan, after the biblical sea monster. But they didn't realize a type of mammoth was already called Leviathan. So it is now often named *Livyatan* – the original Hebrew spelling. The species *Livyatan melvillei* refers to Herman Melville, author of the whaling novel *Moby-Dick*.

UNCOVERING THE PAST

Scientists who study the prehistory of living things are called palaeontologists (pay-lee-on-tol-o-jist). To do this, they work with fossils: the remains of animals and plants preserved in rocks. Fossils of prehistoric sea creatures are often found on land today because many ancient seas have shrunk or disappeared. Also, as the Earth's crust has moved over time, fossils that were once underwater are now on dry land.

There are two types of fossil: body fossils and trace fossils.

Body fossils

preserve the actual parts of an animal or plant. When an animal dies, it may fall into mud or sand, and become covered by another layer of mud or sand. This enables bones, claws and teeth to be preserved, and sometimes soft tissue – and poo. Mud or sand can also harden into rock and retain the shape and form of the body remains as a cast or mould.

Trace fossils

preserve the marks that an animal or plant has left. For example, an animal may have made a burrow, or a plant made holes where its roots once were. Or an animal might have left tracks – this can tell us how fast it moved, and give us clues as to how long its legs were!

How do palaeontologists know how old fossils are? The main technique they use is called stratigraphy. The rocks that contain fossils are formed in flat layers, or strata. Scientists can date the layers of volcanic rock above and below the fossil layers. They do this from the minerals deposited in the volcanic layers.

So, if a layer of volcanic rocks from below the fossil layer is dated at 230 million years, and a volcanic layer above at 240 million years, the age of the fossils must be somewhere between these dates. .

It's a bit like a jigsaw puzzle; the more pieces you fit together, the clearer it becomes.

You don't need to be a professional palaeontologist to discover a dinosaur. You can join fossil-hunting groups instead. A seven-year-old boy from Chile found a new species of dinosaur. His name was Diego Suarez and in 2015 his discovery was named *Chilesaurus diegosuarezi*. So find a fossil of an unknown animal and it could be named after you!

INDEX

The Author

Matthew Rake lives in London, UK, and has worked in publishing for more than 20 years. He has written on a wide variety of topics for adults as well as children, including science, sport and the arts.

The Illustrator

Award-winning illustrator Simon Mendez combines his love of nature and drawing by working as an illustrator with a focus on scientific and natural subjects. He paints on a wide variety of themes but mainly concentrates on portraits and animal subjects. He lives in the United Kingdom.